CORE LANGUAGE SKILLS

Parts of Speech

Kara Murray

PowerKiDS
press.

New York

Published in 2015 by The Rosen Publishing Group, Inc.
29 East 21st Street, New York, NY 10010

First Edition

Editor: Sarah Machajewski
Book Design: Reann Nye

Photo Credits: Cover AVAVA/Thinkstock.com; p. 5 Goodluz/Shutterstock.com; p. 6 Kali Nine LLC/E+/ Getty Images; p. 7 (school) MaxyM/Shutterstock.com; p. 7 (mouse) Szasz-Fabian Jozsef/Shutterstock.com; p. 7 (girl) Samuel Borges Photography/Shutterstock.com; p. 9 Image Source/Digital Vision/Getty Images; pp. 11, 15, 17 (pencil) Julia Ivantsova/Shutterstock.com; p. 13 Guas/Shutterstock.com; p. 19 Jessie Jean/ Taxi/Getty Images.

Library of Congress Cataloging-in-Publication Data

Murray, Kara, author.
 Parts of speech / Kara Murray.
    pages ; cm. — (Core language skills)
 Includes glossary and index.
 ISBN 978-1-4777-7361-1 (pbk.)
 ISBN 978-1-4777-7362-8 (6 pack)
 ISBN 978-1-4777-7360-4 (library binding)
 1. English language—Parts of speech—Juvenile literature. 2. English language—Noun—Juvenile literature. 3. English language—Verb—Juvenile literature. I. Title.
 PE1199.M87 2015
 428.2—dc23
                              2014025936

Manufactured in the United States of America

CPSIA Compliance Information: Batch #CW15PK: For Further Information contact Rosen Publishing, New York, New York at 1-800-237-9932

CONTENTS

WORDS AT WORK

The English language has many words. Every word belongs to a certain group, called a part of speech. There are eight parts of speech. They are nouns, pronouns, adjectives, verbs, adverbs, prepositions, conjunctions, and interjections.

Each word in a sentence has a special job. Parts of speech tell us what a word's job is. A word may name something. It could **describe** something. It may even tell us what action is happening. We use parts of speech every time we read, write, and speak. They're the building blocks of sentences!

Figure It Out

What do parts of speech do?

Find the answer to this question and the others in this book on page 22.

We use the parts of speech every time we write!

5

NOUNS ARE FOR NAMING

A noun is a word that names a person, place, thing, or idea. Anything that exists, whether we can touch it with our hands or only imagine it, has a name. That name is a noun.

There are two kinds of nouns. Common nouns tell us *who* or *what* something is. "Man," "girl," and "doctor" are nouns that tell us who someone is. "School," "mouse," and "garden" are nouns that tell us what something is. Proper nouns name a **specific** person, place, or thing. They're always capitalized, no matter where they are in a sentence.

Raj

Figure It Out

Can you find the common noun and the proper noun in the following sentence? "My friend Raj is always late."

school

girl

mouse

Your first and last name, the name of your city, and the name of your favorite book are all proper nouns. The words "name," "city," and "book" are common nouns. Can you see the difference?

LET THE PRONOUNS HANDLE IT

Pronouns are words that take the place of nouns. The words "he," "she," and "it" are just a few examples. Pronouns give us a way to talk about nouns without always having to use their names.

List of Pronouns

I	it	his
me	its	her
you	we	them
he	us	they
she	our	their

A pronoun must always match the noun it replaces. "I have a lot of video games. It are fun." doesn't make sense, does it? That's because the pronoun "it" doesn't match the noun "video games." You would use the pronoun "they" instead.

Before we can know what a pronoun **refers** to, we must know the noun it's replacing. Look at the following sentences: "I finished my sister's sandwich. She only ate half." It's clear that the pronoun "she" takes the place of the noun "sister." Using the pronoun "she" meant we didn't have to use the noun "sister" twice.

Figure It Out

The sentences below contain nouns and pronouns. One pronoun is underlined. What noun does it refer to? "I love playing basketball. <u>It</u> is a fun sport!"

VERBS IN ACTION

Verbs are words that show action. They tell us what someone or something does. Verbs are important parts of sentences—without them, nothing would happen!

Verbs must *always* agree with the subject of the sentence. If the subject of the sentence is **singular**, or there's only one, the verb must also be singular. If the subject is **plural**, or more than one, the verb must also be plural. To make a singular verb, you often add an "-s" to the end of it. Plural verbs often do not end in "-s."

Figure It Out

In the following sentences, choose the verb that matches the subject of the sentence.

"My dad _____ every night." (cook/cooks)

"These flowers _____ nice." (smell/smells)

"She _____ home from school." (walk/walks)

Verb Tenses

We use verbs to tell about something that's happening now. We can also use verbs to tell about something that happened in the past or something that will happen in the future. This is called verb **tense**.

subject	I	you	he/she/it
present tense	I jump.	You jump.	She jumps.
past tense	I jumped.	You jumped.	She jumped.
future tense	I will jump.	You will jump.	She will jump.

Verbs help us tell about everything we do. Whether you smile, frown, run, skip, or sleep, you always use a verb to say what you're doing.

AWESOME ADJECTIVES

Adjectives are words that describe nouns. Adjectives tell us what someone or something is like. They usually come before the noun they describe. "Pretty," "happy," and "proud" are just a few examples.

Nouns without adjectives can sometimes be boring. The nouns "dress," "baby," and "lion" don't say much on their own. Adding adjectives can really make them shine. Once you read "pretty dress," "happy baby," and "proud lion," you imagine things more clearly!

Adjectives are fun to use in your writing, but don't use too many! It only takes a few to make your writing great.

Figure It Out

The following sentence contains a blank where an adjective can go. Can you fill in the blank with an adjective that describes this dog? "The _____ dog is named Scout."

Choose an adjective based on what the noun is like. You can't describe this dog as "spooky," "tiny," or "dirty," because it's not any of those things!

ADVERBS ARE AMAZING!

There may come a time when you want to describe a verb. One part of speech does just that—adverbs! These adverbs tell us when, where, and how something happened.

We can use adverbs to make our sentences more interesting. If there's a big storm outside, you could say, "The thunder rumbled." Or, you could add an adverb and say, "The thunder rumbled loudly." "Loudly" adds something exciting to the sentence, which makes it more fun to read. Adverbs are commonly used to describe verbs. However, they can describe other parts of speech, too.

Figure It Out

Find the adverbs in the following sentence. "Come home quickly," his grandmother said, "it's going to rain soon."

Kinds of Adverbs

adverbs that describe:

when	where	how
already	upstairs	carefully
during	downstairs	correctly
next	in	easily
now	out	happily
last	underground	quickly
finally	anywhere	slowly
sometimes	here	
soon	there	

There's an easy trick for finding an adverb in a sentence: Look for the word that ends in "-ly!" Many adverbs end in these two letters.

PERFECT PREPOSITIONS

Prepositions are another important part of speech. Prepositions show how nouns and pronouns **relate** to other words in a sentence. Look at the sentence "The pencil is on the desk." The word "on" is the preposition, and it tells us exactly where something is. This is how we know the **relationship** between the pencil and the desk.

Prepositions can also tell us when something happens. Look at the sentence "I brush my teeth before bed." "Before" is the preposition. It tells us when you brush your teeth. Prepositions have a lot of power. Changing them can change your sentence entirely!

Figure It Out

Find the prepositions in the following sentences.
"My bike is behind the garage."
"We'll play after school lets out."

common prepositions

over	under
above	below
on	in
with	through
from	about
to	

Some prepositions on this list can be used as other parts of speech. In these cases, think about what the word's job is. That will tell you what part of speech it is.

CONJUNCTIONS—THE JOINERS

Can't seem to figure out how to bring parts of a sentence together? A conjunction can help you with that. Conjunctions help us join sentences, phrases, and words. The most common conjunctions are "and," "but," "or," "for," "so," and "yet."

"And" is a conjunction that tells you more, such as in the sentence "We went to the beach and swam in the ocean." "But" is a conjunction that makes a **contrast**. Watch how it works in the sentence "I'm sick, but I went to school." Try thinking of some more examples using other conjunctions!

Figure It Out

Can you spot the conjunction in the following sentence? "I want to help you, but I don't know how the machine works."

These girls are at the beach. They're having fun.
Can you combine these sentences using a conjunction?

INTERJECTIONS—WOW!

There's one more part of speech left to learn. Hooray! It's called an interjection, and you just read one. "Hooray" is an interjection. Interjections are parts of speech that state strong **emotions**. They're usually followed by an exclamation point. "Ouch," "yay," "oh," "wow," and "oops" are some interjections you may be familiar with.

All parts of speech are special on their own, but putting them together creates something great. The next time you sit down to write, try adding some adverbs or naming some nouns. It's a great way to build your language skills!

Figure It Out

The following sentences contain all eight parts of speech. Can you find them? "I see tiny ants under our table. Yuck! They are gross, and I truly hate them."

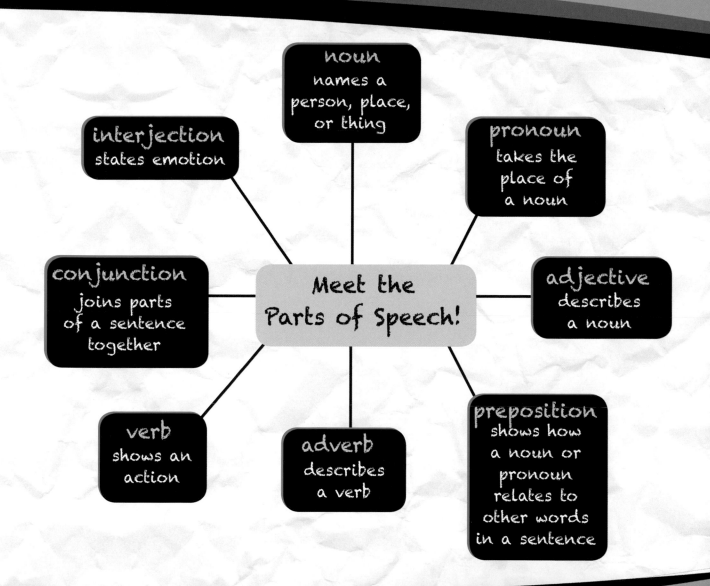

FIGURE IT OUT ANSWERS

Page 4: Parts of speech tell us what a word's job is.

Page 6: The common noun is "friend." The proper noun is "Raj."

Page 9: The pronoun "it" refers to the noun "basketball."

Page 10: "Cooks," "smell," "walks."

Page 12: "Big," "furry," "white," "happy," and "pretty" are just some adjectives you could use.

Page 14: "Quickly" and "soon" are the adverbs.

Page 16: "Behind" and "after" are the prepositions.

Page 18: "But" is the conjunction.

Page 20: Nouns: ants, table; Pronouns: I, our, they, them; Adjectives: tiny, gross; Verbs: see, are, hate; Adverbs: truly; Prepositions: under; Conjunctions: and; Interjections: yuck.

GLOSSARY

contrast (KAHN-traast) The difference between things.

describe (dih-SCRYB) To tell about.

emotion (ih-MOH-shun) Mood or feelings based on something
that happens.

plural (PLUHR-uhl) More than one in number.

refer (rih-FUHR) To have to do with something else.

relate (rih-LAYT) To be connected to something.

relationship (rih-LAY-shun-ship) The state of being connected.

singular (SIHN-gyuh-luhr) One in number.

specific (speh-SIH-fihk) Individual.

tense (TEHNS) The form of the verb that tells when the action happens.

INDEX

WEBSITES

Due to the changing nature of Internet links, PowerKids Press has developed an online list of websites related to the subject of this book. This site is updated regularly. Please use this link to access the list: www.powerkidslinks.com/cls/part